WRITE THIS WAY

WRITING

OUTSTANDING

OPINION PIECES

NANCY LOEWEN

LERNER PUBLICATIONS ◆ MINNEAPOLIS

Lerner Publications Company
A division of Lerner Publishing Group, Inc.
241 First Avenue North
Minneapolis, MN 55401 USA

For reading levels and more information, look up this title at www.lernerbooks.com.

Main body text set in Dante MT Std 12/15. Typeface provided by Monotype.

Library of Congress Cataloging-in-Publication Data

Loewen, Nancy, 1964–
    Writing outstanding opinion pieces / by Nancy Loewen.
        pages cm. — (Write this way)
      ISBN 978-1-4677-7905-0 (lb : alk. paper) — ISBN 978-1-4677-8286-9
(pb : alk. paper) — ISBN 978-1-4677-8287-6 (eb pdf)
      1. Editorials—Authorship—Juvenile literature. I. Title
PN4784.E28L565 2016
808.06'607—dc23   2015000425

Manufactured in the United States of America
1 – VP – 7/15/15

Table of Contents

INTRODUCTION

Quick:
> **What's your favorite TV show?**
> **Who's the best player in the NFL?**
> **Who makes the best french fries?**

Opinions—you have plenty of them. You are constantly observing, evaluating, and making choices and decisions. Your opinions—about everything from your favorite color to the most important social issues of our time—are an essential part of who you are.

Just as you have plenty of opinions, so does everyone else. And we all influence one another, whether we're aware of it or not. If your best friend likes a certain band, you'll give it a listen, right? If your family is always talking politics, you'll probably have plenty to say in a classroom debate. Or maybe you check out a few fashion blogs before you buy new clothes. We think for ourselves, but we also value the opinions of others.

Opinions can be found in all writing genres. People are opinionated by nature, so their views slip out one way or another! But in some forms of writing, expressing opinions is the whole point. Commentaries are short essays in which writers say what they think about topics of public interest. The purpose of a commentary is to offer different viewpoints and promote discussion. Reviews are another essential way people share their opinions. The best reviews contain useful information that others can use to make decisions—about everything from downloading a song to choosing a school.

Many opinion writers help us understand the complexities of politics, international affairs, social justice, and other serious issues. Nicholas Kristof, for example, writes about human rights and world affairs for the *New York Times*. He has won Pulitzer Prizes for his coverage of the explosive political protests that occurred in China's Tiananmen Square in 1989 and the genocide in Darfur, Sudan. Kristof also blogs for the *New York Times* and has more than a million followers on Twitter.

Other opinion writers keep us up to date on lighter subjects, such as sports, music, food, and fashion. Would you like to know if a new TV series is worth your time? Maybe you don't watch anything unless it gets a good score on the movie and TV review site Rotten Tomatoes. Hooked on sports? ESPN writers blog about sports of all kinds, from basketball to horse racing. Are you looking for a little bit of everything? Tavi Gevinson's online magazine, *Rookie*, offers book, music, and movie reviews, along with stories and lots of style.

Opinion writers play a significant role in shaping our culture. We depend on opinion writers to be well informed in their specialty areas and to help us process the vast amount of information that comes our way each day. But one of the coolest things about opinion writing is that you don't have to be a professional writer—or a professional *anything*—to weigh in with your thoughts. Publishing opportunities are abundant, whether in newspapers, magazines, blogs, websites, discussion forums, or social media sites. The audience for an opinion piece could be a few dozen people or many thousands—even millions—of people.

A good opinion piece is like a good conversation: It's lively. It flows well. It introduces new ideas and yet stays on topic. It can be heartfelt or funny—or both. And when it's over, you feel as though you've learned something you wouldn't have learned anywhere else.

In this book, we'll go through the entire process of writing an opinion piece, from coming up with an idea to polishing your final draft. Get ready to tell the world what you think!

DECIDING WHAT TO WRITE ABOUT

Before Internet use became widespread, commentaries were mostly found in print newspapers and magazines. They were often called op-ed pieces because they were printed opposite the editorial page. Now newspapers and magazines publish online editions in addition to the print versions. No matter how people access them, these publications have specific audiences that they're trying to reach. A newspaper might serve a huge metro area or a small town. A magazine might serve people interested in a certain topic, such as politics, entertainment, science, or any number of hobbies. And plenty of organizations that aren't in the business of publishing have websites or newsletters that encourage people to share their views.

So what makes a good commentary? Timeliness is important. Are people talking about the topic? Has new research emerged? Is it something that is affecting people's lives right now? A commentary should be current. That's not to say you can't refer to *any* information from the past. Of course you can! Opinion writers often point out trends that show how our behavior has changed over time and the impact of those changes.

Another major consideration is length. Every publication has its own guidelines, but in general, commentaries are between 300 and 750 words. (That's roughly one to three typed pages.) Commentaries need to be extremely focused, with one main point and evidence to support it.

Effective commentaries often start with a specific incident or example and put it into a larger context. Let's say you want to check out a book at your school library and you can't because the school board has banned it. You could use your experience as a springboard into a discussion about censorship and how it affects students. You might even choose to end the piece with a call to action by asking people to write letters to school board members, sign a petition, or vote for other candidates in the next school board election.

If you're not ready to write a commentary but you still want your voice to be heard, consider writing a letter to the editor. Letters to the editor are usually less than two hundred words. Many people write letters to the editor in direct response to articles that recently appeared in the publication. Often letters to the editor are very personal. A writer might want to publicly thank a person or a group, or make a specific complaint about

WRITE IT OUT!

Make a list of the most interesting people you know. Also write down *why* you think they're so interesting. Do they have unusual hobbies? Do they perform volunteer work for important causes? Have they overcome major challenges in their lives? Maybe your grandfather's friend didn't learn to read until he was an adult, and you think there should be more programs for adult literacy. Or your biology teacher brings to class all sorts of fascinating things from around the world, and you want her to receive recognition for making science come alive for kids. You may find plenty of topics for opinion pieces just by tapping into your own personal connections. As an added bonus, you'll have a ready source of information!

something going on in the writer's neighborhood. Letters to the editor are like a community forum. It's a place where people get together to say what's on their minds.

PICKING A TOPIC

Maybe, for you, deciding what to write about is a no-brainer. You bike everywhere you go, and you think your city should put in more bike lanes. Or maybe your whole family has given up soda, and you want people to be aware of the environmental impact of all those bottles and cans—not to mention the health effects of sipping on lots of sugary drinks. But it's OK if you don't have any ideas right away. You *do* have plenty of opinions worth writing about. You just need to bring them to the surface.

Commentaries focus on current issues, so stay on top of the news—whether it's on TV, in print newspapers or magazines, or online. And this might sound radical, but you could also take a short break from your favorite radio stations or playlists and listen to news radio instead. What stories grab your attention? Which ones do you have strong opinions about? In addition to the news, you could even listen to some of the charismatic media personalities who aren't a bit shy about voicing their opinions on TV, the radio, YouTube, or podcasts. (But remember, they might not have all their facts straight. You'll need to do your own research.)

Does your family contribute to any charities or advocacy organizations? Some examples are the Alzheimer's Association, Mothers Against Drunk Driving (MADD), or the Sierra Club. Check out their websites, blogs, newsletters, or e-mails—you might find all sorts of ideas for an opinion piece. They might even provide you with the names and addresses of publications in your area that accept opinion pieces.

Don Lemon (above) is a journalist for the news network CNN. Watching news broadcasts can help you find current issues to write about in your commentary.

Or try this: For a day or two, bring a small notebook with you wherever you go. Jot down the times you find yourself saying, "I think" or "I don't agree" or "Why can't we do this?" or "We should do that." Or maybe you don't actually say anything out loud, but you wish others knew your thoughts. Write it all down, no matter what it is.

And since you've already got that notebook out anyway, you can also jot down the frustrations you face during the course of your day or week. Were you tardy—again—because it took too long to get through the lunch line? Was the expensive video game you saved your money for a big disappointment? On the flip side, also write down what makes you feel terrific. **Commentaries don't have to be negative. Maybe something is working well and you want to call attention to it.** For example, you and your friends noticed that your grades have improved now that school starts later. A student commentary on school start times could influence school policy in other communities.

LEARN FROM THE MASTERS

Zoocheck is a Canadian charity that works to protect wild animals. Like many organizations, it offers a sample letter to the editor. People who support the Zoocheck cause can use the letter as a model and send their own letters to newspapers and other media outlets in their own communities. Here is an adaptation of that letter:

Dear Editor:

Circuses featuring wild animal acts may seem innocent, but in reality these acts can be cruel and unsafe. I believe they should be banned.

The animals may be penned up in cramped cages for months on end, getting out only for training or performances. They can't behave in a natural way. In addition, many performing animals are large, potentially dangerous species that even zoos often find difficult to house and care for safely. Yet these animals are allowed to perform in circuses, often without adequate protection for staff and audience members.

We should not condone cruelty to animals or animal exploitation by allowing these kinds of acts to visit, nor should we wait for someone to be injured or killed before we decide to act in the interest of human safety. All over the world, cities and even entire countries have banned wild animal acts. Our community should consider a prohibition on wild animal acts as soon as possible.

Sincerely,

[Your name and address]

Record your thoughts without judging them. If you're not comfortable carrying around a notebook, you can keep track of your thoughts in other ways. Send yourself texts or e-mails. Or just sit down once or twice a day and think through the highlights of what you did, said, and observed. Then write down the moments in which you expressed or formed an opinion.

Many of your ideas will be little things that don't seem all that important. That's OK! You need only one solid idea. Generating ideas can be like taking photographs. You might have to take dozens to get the one that really counts. And learning how to pay attention to your thoughts and experiences—and then to connect your ideas to what others may be experiencing—is a useful skill for a writer.

WRITING A REVIEW

The Internet has given just about anyone the chance to be a reviewer—of just about anything! Today on websites and social media, you can review the new fast-food place at the mall and the band performing in someone's basement. You can review the pens you use at school. You can review your new socks! Of course, many of the reviews you see online are written very quickly and may not be well developed or even fair. They might be as short as a sentence or two. Online retailers are always trying to boost the ratings for their products, so they encourage reviews and make it easy to post them. But there's a big difference between a user review on Amazon or Yelp and the more thoughtful and thorough reviews you would find on *Slate* or *Pitchfork*, or in a professional magazine.

People often write reviews because they've had an experience that stands out, either positive or negative. What stands out to you? Did you just finish the best book *ever* and want everyone in the world to read it? Is that pricey makeup you bought not worth the money? Were you blown away by the student art exhibit at the community center?

If nothing jumps out at you, put your daily life under a microscope. What products do you use all the time? What do you do for entertainment? Be methodical about it. Here are some ideas to get you started:

- Media—books, movies, TV shows, podcasts, websites, apps, video games, and music
- Devices—anything electronic, from earbuds to computers
- Clothing—jeans, coats, and shoes
- Sports equipment—baseball gloves, ice skates, and martial arts gear
- Personal care—hair products, makeup, soaps, and cleansers
- Restaurants—local diners, big chains, or even individual food items
- Events—school and community plays, concerts, and other performances
- Exhibits—what's on display at museums, art galleries, libraries, and civic centers

With so many choices, you'll want to be selective. Don't pick a subject if you're not the right audience for it. If you don't watch a lot of sci-fi movies or play a lot of video games, let someone else review those and instead pick something you already know a lot about. Ask yourself: What do I care about most? What knowledge or insight do I have that would be most helpful to other people? Try to find a balance between those two questions. Suppose you're trying to decide between reviewing a popular book you really like and a popular movie you really *dislike* because it stereotypes a group you belong to. You have strong

feelings about both the book and the movie, but if you pick the movie, you would be able to share your own perspective in a deeper way—and make people aware of issues they may not have considered.

Whether you're writing a commentary or a review, what matters most is that you really care about your topic. This is an opinion piece, after all. Don't hold back!

GATHERING YOUR FACTS AND IDEAS

You're writing an opinion piece. Doesn't that mean you can say whatever you want? Well, no—at least, not if you want to be taken seriously. You'll need to explain *why* you hold your opinion. What are your reasons? Try to identify at least three. When you've figured out your reasons, the next step is to find evidence to support them.

GATHERING EVIDENCE

Don't let the word *evidence* make you nervous. You're not on trial! Basically *evidence* is the knowledge or experience you have that forms the basis for your beliefs. You can use hard evidence like facts and statistics, but you can also support your point with stories, examples, quotes, and your own reasoning.

Do you have personal experience with your topic? In more formal types of writing, the personal approach wouldn't be appropriate. **But in opinion writing, you should feel free to share a bit of your life. Telling a brief story makes readers more likely to empathize with you and put themselves in your place.** Let's say you often pick up trash in

Writing about personal experiences can add emotional impact to your commentary. A description of the amount of trash you've cleaned up will help readers empathize with your issue.

your neighborhood. You decide to write a commentary in support of tougher littering laws in your town. A description of all the garbage you pick up—and your feelings about it   would get people to pay attention.

Examples help you get your meaning across too. A good example reinforces a concept that you have already explained, or it might even take the place of a more complicated description. If you're writing about the impact of big-box stores in your town, you would want to name a few of these stores (Walmart, Target, K-Mart, Home Depot, and others) so your audience would know exactly the type of stores you're talking about. You could also describe a specific instance of a big-box store putting a smaller store out of business and how that affected individual families as well as the community.

Quotes from experts are another way to support your opinion. They give you authority! Quotes demonstrate that you are not the only one who holds this opinion—someone who knows a lot about this issue shares your opinion as well. You can quote ordinary people too, if they've been affected by the topic you're writing about. For example, if you're writing a piece about the Make-a-Wish Foundation (which grants wishes to children with life-threatening medical conditions), you could quote a child or a family member who had a memorable experience thanks to the program. Or you could quote an official who runs the program. Or you could include both!

LEARN FROM THE MASTERS

Even if you're writing about difficult, far-reaching topics, don't shy away from the personal angle. Stories and examples, whether from your own life or someone else's, can engage the reader's emotions and help you create a memorable piece. Colbert I. King is a Pulitzer Prize-winning columnist for the *Washington Post*, specializing in urban and national affairs. In "Helping Children Feel Safe Is a Community Effort," he reminds readers that racial unrest and violence have a deep impact on children—a fact that is often overlooked in news stories. If kids are scared and under stress, they can't learn. King knows this from personal experience, having been traumatized by a couple of violent incidents that occurred in his own neighborhood while he was growing up. He also describes a boy's request from a letter to Santa program: "I just wanna be safe." King then implores caring adults to devote time to children in troubled circumstances.

Another powerful way to support your point is with statistics. Often numbers speak louder than words. Compelling statistics help you make your case. The key here is *compelling*. Choose statistics that are easy to understand and even a bit surprising. They should get at the heart of your argument. Be sure to provide the context that makes the statistic meaningful. Answering questions like these can help your reader understand why the statistic is important:

- **Is the number up or down from previous years?**
- **Are experts concerned about what the numbers mean?**
- **Are the numbers an exception, or do they signify a trend?**

You can use your own observations and reasoning as evidence in your opinion piece as well. If you want to share your thoughts about your community swimming pool, for example, you could compare your pool to the pools of other towns near you. You wouldn't need expert testimony or statistics to do that. Or maybe you've noticed that students are restless in school on days when you have morning assemblies, and you think your school should schedule assemblies in the afternoon instead. Go ahead and speculate about the advantages of afternoon assemblies. If your reasons are logical and clearly stated, your readers will follow along.

The kind of evidence you use depends on the nature of your piece. In a book review, you'd want to include excerpts from the book and plenty of your own reflections. In a piece on juvenile detention, you'd definitely want to include some statistics and expert testimony. **The better you understand your own reasons for your opinion, the easier it will be to select the right kind of evidence.** So take a little time at the beginning to really think things through.

RESEARCHING YOUR TOPIC

To track down evidence for your piece, you might have to do some research. But don't let that word scare you. Research can be fun. After all, you care enough about your topic to write about it. Wouldn't you like to learn a little more?

There are plenty of choices: books, newspapers, magazines, blogs, podcasts, documentaries, TV news segments, and so on. In fact, you might find so much material that you don't know where to begin! To avoid information overload in your Internet searches, use specific words instead of general ones. When you do find a useful article, be on the lookout for additional terms that could help you refine your search. Finally, don't forget that you have an assistant at the library—your reference librarian.

It's very important to choose credible sources. Universities, government organizations, and reputable magazines and newspapers are good places to start. If you're not sure a

Newspapers are a good source for both topic ideas and research. For example, a news article might provide statistics that you can use in your commentary. Just be sure to cite the source in your piece.

magazine or a newspaper is credible, check a website called NewsTrust (newstrust.net). It rates all sorts of news sources for trustworthiness. It is updated daily, and it can help you figure out if you should rely on the source you found. If you're considering blogs and other content created by individuals, look for solid author credentials, such as advanced degrees, publication credits, and career experience. Whatever your source, be sure you know when it was published—you don't want to use outdated information!

Whether you consult lots of sources or just a few, be sure to write them down. You may even want to write a formal bibliography. Then you'd need to record the title, the author, the place of publication (or the web address for websites), the publisher, the date of publication, and the page number. That way, when it's time to cite your sources in your piece, you won't have to scramble.

DOCUMENTING YOUR SOURCES

As you do your research, you'll want to take notes. It pays to be organized with those too. You can use a computer program, a notebook, or note cards—whatever you prefer. The main thing is to know where you found each piece of information. Backtracking through all your reading to find a certain statistic or quote is no fun!

Here's a tip about taking notes: Unless you are using a direct quote, don't write word for word. Summarize the key points instead. That way you won't unintentionally plagiarize. Plagiarizing—passing off another person's words or original ideas as your own—is a form of stealing. Plagiarism is easy to detect online. Even if it's done accidentally, it can ruin a writer's reputation and credibility.

Libel is another issue to be aware of. Libel means to publish misleading or untrue statements about someone, with the intent of harming that person's reputation. Libel is illegal. Whether people are celebrities or ordinary Joes, if they have been negatively affected by the publication of false statements, they have the right to take the matter to court. But don't let concerns about libel keep you from expressing yourself! As long as you use reliable sources and take accurate notes, you'll be fine.

During research, don't limit yourself to material that's already been published. Why not conduct your own interview to give your readers something entirely new? If you know people who would have something meaningful to say about your topic, explain your project and ask them to share their thoughts. Most people will be

WRITE IT OUT!

Conduct your own original research to make your opinion piece stand out. In addition to interviews, you could create a survey (on paper or online) to find out how others in your community feel about your topic. For example, if you think your school places too much emphasis on sports, you could survey the students, teachers, and parents at your school. Ask if they agree or disagree with your opinion, and ask for their comments.

Observing the field is another way to conduct original research. In a piece about the need for good manners, for instance, you could watch people going in and out of a building's public entrance and observe how often people hold the door open for the person behind them.

flattered and want to help. Even experts you don't know might be willing to talk to you on the phone or do an e-mail interview. It never hurts to ask!

GATHERING INFORMATION FOR A REVIEW

When you're writing a review, you won't need to do a lot of research (although you *should* double-check any facts you use). But you'll need to thoroughly explore your own thoughts. Often we know if we like something or not, but pinpointing exactly why we feel that way isn't always so easy.

Brainstorming comes in handy here. Without stopping to evaluate your thoughts or put them in any kind of order, write down all of your observations about your subject. Really zero in on your reactions. Here are some examples of the type of questions to ask yourself:

- **Which scene in your book had you turning pages as fast as you could?**
- **Was it hard to figure out your video game at first?**
- **If you watched a movie a second or third time, at what point did you decide you could go get popcorn without missing anything?**

Keep brainstorming, even when you think you've got plenty of ideas. If you keep at it long enough, you might surprise yourself with ideas you weren't consciously aware of.

If brainstorming isn't your thing, try making a list of pros and cons. What did you like about what you're reviewing? What didn't you like? If some of your ideas don't seem to fit in either column, make a third column of other observations. Some of them might find their way into your piece later on.

ANALYZE YOUR THOUGHTS

Once you've written everything down, start thinking analytically. Do certain ideas go together? Maybe you realize that a band's new album seemed boring to you because it was too much like their previous one. Or you thought the special effects made a movie worth seeing, even though the sound track was terrible and the story fell apart in the second half. Keep sifting and sorting your ideas, and eventually a pattern will emerge. But don't feel as though you have to include *everything* in your review. Just stick to the points that seem most important to you.

With reviews, keep in mind that you also need to describe the subject of your review for a reader who hasn't seen or

WRITE IT OUT!

You can quickly pick up on the dos and don'ts of reviews just by examining some reviews online. Pick a book or a movie you're interested in but don't know much about. Then look at reviews on a variety of websites and blogs. Read through the reviews, and with each one, ask yourself these questions:

- What did this review tell me about this book?

- What did it tell me about the person writing the review?

- How might it affect my decision to read this book or watch this movie?

Take notes about what worked and what didn't.

experienced it. This can get tricky, especially with books or movies. Whatever you do, don't give away the ending! Don't try to include every last detail of the plot. Focus on what the reader absolutely has to know to understand your review. If you are reviewing a product, be sure to include all the relevant information, such as brand and model number. On the other hand, don't let your description dominate your review. Your audience doesn't want to read a summary that could have been written by anyone. **The whole point of a review is to share what *you* think, so make that your focus. Be sure that you're writing about your own experience.** For example, if you're reviewing a popular app, don't simply repeat what your friends say about it—write about how it worked for you personally.

Also, keep in mind that you should always be respectful. Even if you're writing a very negative review, remember that someone put a lot of effort into creating whatever it is you're reviewing.

CHAPTER 3

PREPARING TO WRITE

You've gathered all sorts of ideas, but it's not *quite* time to write. Before jumping in, it pays to consider your strategy—and to know a little more about where your piece is headed. You've heard of creative visualization, right? Athletes often use it to improve their performance. They imagine themselves making free throws or sticking the landing on the vault. If they visualize what they want to happen, it will be more likely to happen. It's the same way with writing. You'll end up with a better piece if you have a clear vision of what you want to accomplish.

FIGURING OUT YOUR STRUCTURE

First, consider structure. An opinion piece isn't an essay that unfolds gradually, with the most persuasive argument at the end. It's not like a long-distance race, in which a runner conserves energy for the final stretch. An opinion piece is more like a sprint. The starter gun goes off—and you zip along at full speed the entire way, focused on that finish line.

Like any good piece of writing, your piece should have a beginning, a middle, and an end. This might seem obvious, but it doesn't happen automatically. Have you ever read a piece that rambled on and on and didn't seem to have a point? Readers

will quickly tune you out if your piece doesn't seem to be going anywhere.

The beginning, or the introduction, needs to accomplish two goals: to grab your reader's attention and to let your reader know what your piece is about. As you prepare to write, try to think of a catchy phrase, a surprising statistic, or a short anecdote that would be a good lead-in to your topic. But if nothing comes to mind right away, don't worry about it. You can always figure that out later. Right now it's more important to figure out your main point—your opinion, in other words! A clearly worded opinion statement sets the tone for the rest of your piece and makes it easier to figure out your supporting points. You want your readers to know exactly where you stand. Here are a few examples:

- Memorial Park needs water fountains that work.
- Schools should offer students time each day to read for pleasure.
- Fans of *How to Train Your Dragon* will love *How to Train Your Dragon 2*.

Next comes the middle, or the body. Here you present the reasons for your opinion and the evidence to back it up. Journalists use a structure called the inverted pyramid. That means putting your most important points first. This way, people can get the gist of an article even if they don't read all the way to the end.

WRITE IT OUT!

To learn how to write attention-getting leads and thought-provoking conclusions, study the work of the pros. Look at the editorial pages of a large newspaper and figure out what techniques the writers used. Then copy your favorite leads and conclusions by hand. The simple act of writing them out—as if they were your own thoughts—will give you a deeper understanding of concepts such as rhythm, pacing, sentence structure, and word choice. This will make it easier for you to recognize if your own work is effective or not.

The end, or the conclusion, pulls everything together. If your piece were a math problem, the conclusion would be the answer—the *right* answer, given with confidence! Try not to include new information in the conclusion. Instead, summarize or restate what you've already said and pay special attention to your last few lines. Make them as powerful as they can be. Consider closing with a quote or a brief story, or go full circle by repeating a phrase or an image that appears in the introduction.

CREATING AN OUTLINE

While your opinion piece should be a quick, focused read for your audience, the writing process itself isn't a sprint. You can take your time with that! **Whether your piece will be long or short, making an outline is a good strategy. It doesn't need to be a formal outline with a complicated system of numbers and letters. An outline can be a simple list, a diagram, or even a bunch of thought bubbles!** As long as it helps you organize your material in logical order, anything goes.

When you have arranged your points so it's easy to see them at a glance, examine them closely. One common mistake is trying to support your points with a variation of what you just said, instead of providing new information. For example, in a review of a video game, you might say that the graphics are realistic. If you support this by saying that the graphics are lifelike, isn't that the same thing?

Another common mistake is to jump to conclusions. That happens when you form your opinion without knowing all the facts. Most of us have experienced this in our personal lives. Have you ever thought a friend was mad at you, but it turned out she just didn't feel well or was upset about something else? You based your opinion on a little bit of evidence, without considering

WRITE IT OUT!
Are you the kind of writer who likes to dive right in? Would you rather write off the top of your head than outline? Then do it! Just write your piece in whatever way it comes out. Don't stop to correct anything. When you're done, outline what you've already got. Then review your outline, revise it, and use it as a guide for your next draft.

other explanations for her behavior. Don't let that happen in your writing. If you want to make a solid case—even if you're just reviewing a costume for your dog—you should take a step back and see if you're overlooking anything.

ESSENTIALS OF GOOD WRITING

While structure is very important, it's not the whole story. A perfectly structured commentary still might not make any impact on readers. So before you get started, let's take a look at the basics of good, solid writing. You'll want to remember these suggestions when you start writing your first draft.

Your readers will pick up on diction right away. *Diction* means "word choice"—or rather, the total effect of *all* of your word choices. Diction ranges from formal to slang. Formal diction is used mostly in academic or legal writing, and it may contain big words and complicated sentences. Slang, on the other hand, is very casual and may include new words that aren't yet in common use. You probably use slang when you're talking to your friends. **When you're writing, choose the level of diction that's right for your audience. For most commentaries, you'd want to be a little more formal than you would for a blog post written for an audience of your peers.**

If you really want your writing to pop, keep it lean. Use strong, precise nouns and verbs, and don't rely too much on adjectives or adverbs. For example, instead of running quickly, a person could dash or bolt or sprint. A small bird could be a finch or a sparrow. That blue sweater you're reviewing could be indigo or ultramarine. Choices like these will energize your writing and make it more specific.

You might be thinking this is an awful lot of work just to speak your mind! But remember that you can use the skills you're learning now in a wide range of writing projects in the future. When you have a firm grasp of the basics, the possibilities are limitless.

WRITING YOUR
FIRST DRAFT (OR TWO)

So far you've picked your topic, gathered information, outlined your main points and supporting evidence, and reviewed the essentials of strong writing. What's next? You guessed it. It's time to write your first draft.

Maybe you've already developed your own writing process. You like to dash out a draft as quickly as you can while listening to music and eating a snack. Maybe you like to go somewhere quiet and take your time with every sentence. You might prefer to work in short sessions or in one long stretch of time. If a certain approach seems to work for you, go ahead and stick with it. But feel free to experiment with other approaches if you think it's time to try something different. Ask your friends or teachers what works best for them, or look up your favorite authors online to see if they've discussed their writing process in a blog post or an interview.

No matter how you approach writing your first draft, keep this in mind: It doesn't have to be perfect. First drafts are nothing more than a starting point. The most important thing about a first draft is that you did it. So don't pressure yourself.

Once you've written everything you want to say (at least for now), take a break. Even an hour or two away will help clear your

WRITE IT OUT!

If you're having trouble getting started with your first draft, try this approach: Look at all the points in your outline. For each one, add a few words. Then go through the outline again and add a few more words. Eventually you'll move from phrases to sentences and from sentences to paragraphs.

head so that you'll be able to see things more clearly when you return. That's just how the human mind works. When you're creating, you can't possibly focus on everything at once. But if you go on and do other things, you'll be able to look at the piece as a whole when you come back to it.

At this point, focus on structure rather than on smaller details that can easily be changed later. Your structure is like the skeleton of your piece, defining its shape and supporting all the ideas that are in it. Even if your piece is very short, structure counts. So when you've written a solid draft or two, ask yourself these questions:

- Does your piece have a definite beginning, middle, and end?
- Do you clearly state your opinion?
- Have you supported it with evidence?

You might be wondering why it's necessary to double-check all this. You did make an outline, after all. But often people write whatever words come to mind, and they don't follow their outlines as closely as they thought they would. That's OK—it happens all the time. But then you need to reevaluate. Are you still heading to the same goal? Do you need to make a course correction? Or possibly, in the process of writing, you discovered a whole new line of thinking that's even better than what you intended originally. Go with it! That's another cool thing about writing. It helps us figure out what we really think.

For now, don't worry about how long your piece is. Most writers write more than they need, and they start cutting only near the end of the revision process. It's much easier to cut than it is to add. Maybe you start out writing a letter to the editor, but you have so much to say that you decide to write a commentary instead. Or the short review you intended for a certain website will turn into a much longer piece that you can publish elsewhere as a blog post.

CITING SOURCES

Do you still have that bibliography handy? How about those note cards? If your piece includes the ideas of others, you need to credit your sources. This applies to quotes, statistics, and any lines of thought that you didn't actually come up with yourself. Be sure to include all the pertinent information. If you're quoting an expert, it's not enough to say the expert's name—you have to let the reader know what qualifications this person has that relate to your topic. If you are using statistics, you have to tell the reader which organization gathered those numbers and for what period of time. Often the words *according to* are used to give credit. Here are some forms that attributions can take:

> According to Sam Smith, president of the Springfield Rotary Club, the new park will open on July 1.

> "The new park will open on July 1," said Sam Smith, president of the Springfield Rotary Club.

> The United States Department of Agriculture reports that Americans consumed more than 1.8 billion pounds of green beans for Thanksgiving dinner in 2013.

> In 2013 Americans consumed more than 1.8 billion pounds of green beans for Thanksgiving dinner, as reported by the United States Department of Agriculture.

These examples show how citations might look in your piece. But that's only part of the story. Keep track of all your sources, whether or not you need to cite them in your piece. Newspapers, magazines, and respected websites have a reputation to uphold and may decide not to publish your piece if they can't verify the accuracy of your information.

IF YOU GET STUCK

You had a good start, but now the words aren't coming. Or else your ideas are so disorganized, writing feels like chasing papers that are blowing in the wind. You have writer's block—but don't worry. Almost every writer experiences writer's block at some point, and you *will* get through it. If possible, take a break from your writing. Do something else. Listen to music, walk your dog, call a friend—or take a nap! When you come back to your piece, you may find that the words are flowing again.

If taking a break doesn't do the trick, try moving on to a different part of your piece. Skip the part that's causing trouble and go to a section you're more enthusiastic about. There's no reason you have to write in the same order as your outline. Or if the problem is that you're trying to do too much at once, put your blinders on and focus on one very small step. Revise a single sentence or change a single word. Then take another small step. Keep doing that, and you may find yourself on a roll before too long.

If you encounter writer's block, try taking a walk to give your mind a break.

FINDING YOUR VOICE

Once you're good to go on the structure of your piece, you can play around with some writing techniques that will give your piece flair. You may have already used these techniques in what you've written so far. But if not, ask yourself if you could strengthen your piece by using elements such as humor, metaphorical language, or repetition.

Unless the overall tone of your piece is very serious, humor is definitely an option. Humor can show a reader what's going on beneath the surface of an issue, and it's a great way to hold the reader's attention. There are a lot of ways to add humor to your piece. You could include a funny quote or story. You could add an over-the-top exaggeration. You could use irony, in which you say the opposite of what you mean. Be open to using humor and see what happens. If it works, it works—and if it doesn't, that's OK too. Just be sure that your use of humor enhances your meaning instead of detracting from it.

Metaphors and similes are comparisons that show how two different things are similar. Like examples, they tap into your reader's intuition. A simile uses *like* or *as* in its comparison. A metaphor doesn't use *like* or *as*. It simply says something *is* something else.

Simile: These athletic shoes made me feel as if I were walking on air.

Metaphor: Wearing these athletic shoes, I was walking on air.

Metaphors and similes can liven up your writing, but they can also weigh your writing down if you use too many. Also, remember that many metaphors and similes are idioms—expressions that don't make sense literally but are understood by people of a particular culture. "She eats like a bird" is an example of an idiom. If your audience includes a lot of people for whom English isn't a native language, avoid using this sort of comparison.

Repetition sets up expectations and pulls the reader in. Repeating certain words or phrases, even in a short piece, puts your reader on alert. The reader recognizes that a word or a phrase has been repeated and will pay extra attention to it. Public speakers use repetition to good effect, and it works well in writing

LEARN FROM THE MASTERS

Some opinion writers use humor to make serious points. In "Nap Time Has Been Cancelled. A Follow-Up Letter to Career-Ready Kindergarteners," *Washington Post* columnist Alexandra Petri writes about the growing trend of putting academic pressure on young children. She describes a kindergarten class of the future, in which the traditional activities of kindergarten are replaced with ones that will prepare kids for their careers. "Never, at any point, in the workplace will Jacob be required to stand behind a clump of 5-year-olds and pretend to be a sunflower," she notes.

In her scenario, kids take coffee breaks instead of playing outside at recess. Story time is now résumé-building time. Finger painting is finger pointing. Kids who throw tantrums won't get a time-out—they'll get a contract for a reality show instead. The situation is funny and absurd but very effective in getting across Petri's message that kids should be allowed to be kids.

too. If you were writing about the disastrous consequences of an oil spill, for instance, you could name different animals:

The oil spill is having a devastating impact on the ocean's wildlife. The dolphins are dying. The pelicans are dying. The turtles are dying. The oysters are dying.

You could use the repetition in one paragraph or scattered throughout your entire piece. That simple structure, repeated, adds a sense of drama and sadness that readers will respond to.

Remember that it's entirely up to you how many drafts you write. Every writer has a different process. Some accomplished authors write dozens of drafts! The reader isn't going to know—or care—how long you took to write your piece. What matters is that you said what you needed to say.

CHAPTER 5

WRAPPING IT UP

Writing is a complex combination of creating and revising. When you write your first or second draft, you're mostly creating. You can't be too critical of yourself at this point, or you'll never write anything! With later drafts, you're mostly revising. It's true that creative inspiration could strike at any time. Suddenly the ideal ending just pops into your head, or you come across a quote that makes your point perfectly. But it's also true that the further along you are in the process, the more analytical you should be.

REVISING YOUR PIECE

At this point, make sure that your content is solid and that you've included everything you intended to. Here's a quick checklist:

- Have you taken a clear stand on your topic? Is your main point easily identified?
- Are the reasons for your opinion clearly explained? Have you provided evidence from examples, quotes, statistics, stories, or your own observations and reasoning?
- Have you properly credited your sources for statistics, quotes, or important ideas that aren't your own?

- Does your introduction have a hook that will pull readers in?
- Does your conclusion bring your piece to a satisfying and definite end?
- Have you adequately explained words or ideas that are unique to your topic?

If you're good to go on these elements, it's time to look at your piece sentence by sentence. First, ask yourself if anything can be cut. When working in creative mode, it's easy to overlook parts that are wordy or awkward. In editing mode, however, check for any word or phrase that doesn't serve a purpose. Don't worry—this doesn't mean stripping out all the good stuff. Opinion writing is personal and conversational, so there's room for a few extra words if they convey your style. But with every sentence you read, ask yourself: Is there a better way to say this? Can I get rid of anything and still get my meaning across?

WRITE IT OUT!

Here's an exercise to make sure your writing doesn't contain a lot of filler. Go through your piece line by line and remove all the adjectives and adverbs you can find. How does your piece read without them? Then go through it again, adding back only the adjectives and adverbs that are necessary. Exchange your work with a friend or two and see if you agree which words belong and which ones don't.

As you are reviewing your work, carefully examine the structure of your sentences. If you use the same structure repeatedly, your writing becomes monotonous and predictable. Pay especially close attention to the first words of your sentences, and change them up so you're not repeating the same opening words in close succession.

Also, watch out for passive sentences. In these, the subject isn't taking action but is being acted upon. *"The cat was chased by the dog"* is an example. A better choice would be *"The dog chased the cat."* Here the dog is the subject and is taking action. Both sentences have the same meaning, but the second one is more direct and active.

Sometimes writers use passive sentences when they don't have all their facts or don't want to assign blame. For example, "The tree was cut down" doesn't say *who* cut down the tree. (You'll find a lot of passive sentences in the political world!) But don't think you have to avoid *all* passive sentences. On rare occasions, a passive sentence is less awkward than an active one if it allows you to emphasize a certain idea.

Also, consider how your piece flows. Ideally, your ideas are closely connected, allowing readers to take one small step after another. If your piece has big gaps, look at your transitions. You may need to add a sentence or two to show how one idea is related to another. These transition sentences can be important additions to your piece, helping your readers to follow your line of thinking. But sometimes just a few words can accomplish this. Signal words alert the reader to what's ahead. They aren't the most exciting words, but they do an important job. Here are some examples:

Continuation: one reason, also, likewise, next, another

Change of direction: although, even though, but, however

Sequence: first, next, before, until, after, then

Illustrate: for example, for instance

Emphasis: especially, most of all, the main point

Conclusion: as a result, consequently, finally

THINKING ABOUT TITLES

Everything is coming together, and you're in the home stretch. Take a few moments to think about the first thing your readers will see: your title. A good title tells readers what your piece is about in a brief but lively way. Read your piece and see if any phrases really stand out to you. If you have a few favorites, could you combine them in some way? Can you think of a common saying that could be adapted to your topic? In many organizations, staff members write the titles of the pieces that are published—but it doesn't hurt to include your own, just in case they want to use it!

PROOFREADING

Maybe you've noticed that in this entire discussion of revision, we haven't yet touched on spelling, grammar, or punctuation. That's because there's a big difference between revising and proofreading. Revising is what you've done so far. It involves thinking at a very high level. Revising is about your ideas and how you express them.

Proofreading, on the other hand, is about following the accepted conventions of writing. While your ideas are what count the most, proofreading is still important. A piece filled with spelling mistakes or grammatical errors won't be taken seriously. Right or wrong, readers may assume that if you don't care about proofreading your work, you probably don't care about accuracy or fairness either. Besides, mistakes are distracting. Readers might focus on the errors and not get the full impact of your best ideas.

REFLECTIONS FROM THE FIELD

Andy Ihnatko is a technology journalist for the *Chicago Sun-Times*. He acknowledges that writing can be a challenge—and advises writers to take pride in their finished work. "Every writer seeks one of those effortless days in which it seems like you just go into a trance, and the thread keeps revealing itself as fast as you can pull it," he says. But he also acknowledges that this rarely happens. Obstacles are inevitable, and it's the writer's job to find a way around them. "Writing is *hard*," Ihnatko says. "That's why so few people stick to it and actually *finish* things. It's also why you have a right to be immensely proud when you finish something."

Andy Ihnatko (above) takes a photo of an iPad to include with his review of the device in 2010.

Read through your piece as many times as you need to, concentrating on different aspects each time through. And get input from other people. When you've worked on a piece for a long time, it's common to develop blind spots. You've read the same words over and over, and it's easy to miss even obvious mistakes. But someone who is reading the piece for the first time may be able to point out places that still need a little work.

To get the most meaningful feedback, ask your reader specific questions. You may even want to share a checklist of questions like the ones provided on pages 38 and 39. This isn't about seeking compliments—it's about making your piece the best it can be. **With every comment you receive, ask yourself: Do I agree with this point? How can I address this reader's concerns?** If you have an open mind but you still disagree with your reader, don't feel you have to change anything. You are the writer, and you get final say.

THE NEXT STEP

You've written a great opinion piece, and you want to share it with others. Why keep it to yourself? Maybe you already know exactly where you'd like to publish it. It might be the local newspaper or a website you enjoy. It might be a contest.

Wherever you plan to send it, make sure you know and understand the submission guidelines. And definitely familiarize yourself with the publication you intend to submit to. Read the work that's already been published and decide if your piece would fit in or if you should try somewhere else.

It's exciting to think of sharing your work with lots of people. But be aware that publishing can be very competitive. Rejection is a part of the process. In the world of professional writing, virtually *all* writers have had their work turned down—many times! A rejection doesn't mean your piece is terrible or that you're a bad writer. Most likely, it just means that the editors simply liked other pieces a little more or that another writer's topic was a better fit for the publication's needs at that time. Editors may receive dozens and even hundreds more submissions than they can accept. A rejection isn't anything to be ashamed of. In fact, you should be proud, because it means you're trying! If your topic is still relevant, send your piece somewhere else. And then get going on your next one.

Let's say you do publish an opinion piece. Congratulations! Your opinion is out there for many people to see. If your piece is online, there may be places for readers to comment. Not everyone will agree with you, so be prepared for some negative comments. Don't take them personally, though—it's just not worth it.

On the other hand, some readers might bring up issues you hadn't considered. You could start a debate. You might even be persuaded to change your mind!

That's how this whole opinion-sharing business works. We all influence one another. Opinions that are arrived at hastily and clung to rigidly aren't worth much. But if we are honest, thoughtful, and passionate, forming and sharing our opinions can make us better people—and help us all create a better world.

WRITING FOR A LIVING

Maybe you've discovered that opinion writing is a natural fit for you. You enjoy exploring your own thoughts and find research to be fun and rewarding. You could be a professional opinion writer—and the best part is, there are lots of things you can do on your own to start your training.

If you're hoping to make a living as a reviewer, you'll also need a lot of knowledge in a particular area. If you want to be a movie critic, for example, watch a lot of movies! In addition, you should read reviews written by highly regarded movie critics. You should learn about movie history, filming techniques, the various genres, and so on. Whether your passion is movies, technology, music, fashion, books, food, or anything else, you can do a lot to prepare for a future career as an opinion writer.

Maybe you'd like to write commentaries on social issues. You can prepare for that kind of career by getting involved with organizations you support. Volunteer in as many ways as you can. The more hands-on experience you have in your area of interest, the better. And get used to putting your ideas out there, whether it's starting a spirited discussion in the school cafeteria or using social media to spread the word.

Some columnists begin their careers as journalists. They spend many years reporting the news objectively, without expressing their personal opinions at all. Then they decide they want to share their own views, so they begin writing commentaries. Because these writers know the issues so well, readers respect them and trust what they have to say.

If you're interested in journalism, begin by writing for your school newspaper or by contributing to your local paper. Save everything you publish and build your portfolio.

Another path you could take is to major in one of the social sciences (such as history, political science, economics, anthropology, and sociology). This would give you credibility and qualify you for many types of jobs with a writing component. And remember that many opinion writers don't start out as writers at all but have fully developed careers in other areas. They may publish articles and books for people in their own industry. If they have a knack for writing about specialized topics in a way people can relate to, they may go on to write books and columns for a general audience.

The skills that make someone a terrific opinion writer can also be used in other writing occupations. You could be an advertising copywriter or a web content developer. You could make documentaries. You could work in public relations. You could be a lobbyist, trying to convince public officials to take a certain position on an issue.

Remember that opinion writing isn't all or nothing. You don't have to do it full-time. Lots of people publish reviews or commentaries as freelancers. They're not employed by the publisher and they probably won't make a ton of money, but they do it because they believe their opinions matter. And if you write your own blog, you can be completely in control and build your own following. Who knows where that might lead?

SOURCE NOTES

10   "Sample Letter to the Editor," Zoocheck Canada, accessed
       December 2, 2014, http://www.zoocheck.com/circuses
       /lettertoeditor.pdf.

13   Suzette Martinez Standring, *The Art of Opinion Writing:*
       Insider Secrets from Top Op-Ed Columnists (Richmond, KY:
       RRP International, 2014), 138.

16   Colbert I. King, "Helping Children Feel Safe Is a
       Community Effort," *Washington Post*, January 2, 2015,
       http://www.washingtonpost.com/opinions/colbert-king
       -helping-children-feel-safe-is-a-community-effort/2015
       /01/02/d91ea0de-91fc-11e4-a900-9960214d4cd7_story.html.

25   Mario-Francisco Robles, "Film Review: 'Interstellar,'"
       Latino-Review, November 5, 2014, http://www.latino
       -review.com/news/film-review-interstellar.

32   Tracy Clayton and Heben Nigatu, "39 Pieces of Advice for
       Journalists and Writers of Color," *BuzzFeed*, July 21, 2014,
       http://www.buzzfeed.com/hnigatu/advice-for-journalists
       -and-writers-of-color#.kyr66X1GJY.

33 "Thanksgiving by the Numbers," US Department of
    Agriculture, accessed December 10, 2014, http://www.nass
    .usda.gov/Newsroom/2014/thanksgiving_by_the_
    numbers.pdf.

36 Alexandra Petri, "Nap Time Has Been Cancelled. A
    Follow-Up Letter to Career-Ready Kindergarteners,"
    Washington Post, April 28, 2014, http://www
    .washingtonpost.com/blogs/compost/wp/2014/04/28
    /nap-time-has-been-cancelled-a-follow-up-letter-to-career
    -ready-kindergarteners/.

42 Andy Ihnatko, "There Is No Such Thing as Writer's Block,"
    Andy Ihnatko's Celestial Waste of Bandwidth (blog), October
    7, 2011, http://ihnatko.com/2011/10/07/there-is-no
    -writers-block/.

GLOSSARY

advocacy: the act of supporting a cause

anecdote: a short description of something that happened

bibliography: a detailed list of the sources an author consulted while writing a work

cite: to briefly note the source of a particular piece of information

compelling: holding one's attention; powerful and convincing

editorial: a commentary representing the opinion of an organization's publisher, editor, or editorial board

guidelines: a set of instructions that explains how a particular organization wants things done

relevant: directly related to the subject at hand

transition: a word or phrase that links ideas, allowing the reader to pass from one idea to the next

SELECTED BIBLIOGRAPHY

Bunyi, Angela. "Exploring the Genre of Review Writing." Scholastic. Accessed November 20, 2014. http://www.scholastic.com /teachers/lesson-plan/exploring-genre-review-writing.

Fink, Conrad C. *Writing Opinion for Impact.* Ames: Iowa State University Press, 1999.

McLain, John. "How to Write a Strong Opinion Piece." Write to Done. Accessed November 11, 2014. http://writetodone.com/how-to -write-a-strong-opinion-piece-for-your-blog/.

"Op-Eds and Letters to the Editor." Communications Consortium Media Center. Accessed November 11, 2014. http://www.ccmc.org /node/16179.

Peterson, Louis J. "How to Write Personal Essays and Opinion Pieces." *PoeWar* (blog), August 29, 2014. http://www.poewar.com/having -your-say-writing-personal-essays/.

Shapiro, Susan. "10 Rules for Writing Opinion Pieces." *Writer's Digest,* July 29, 2009. http://www.writersdigest.com/writing-articles /by-writing-goal/improve-my-writing/10-rules-for-writing -opinion-pieces.

Standring, Suzette Martinez. *The Art of Opinion Writing: Insider Secrets from Top Op-Ed Columnists.* Richmond, KY: RRP International, 2014.

"Tips for Writing Great Reviews." Google+. Accessed November 12, 2014. https://support.google.com/plus/answer/2519605?hl=en.

FURTHER INFORMATION

Bodden, Valerie. *Write and Revise Your Project*. Minneapolis: Lerner Publications, 2015. All the bases are covered in this book, from developing a convincing argument to writing a strong conclusion.

Creative Kids Magazine
http://www.ckmagazine.org/submissions
This online magazine for kids ages eight to sixteen publishes all kinds of creative work, including editorial essays.

Dogo Media
http://www.dogonews.com
Dogo Media is an online community of kids and educators. In addition to news, the site features book, movie, and website reviews by and for kids from kindergarten to twelfth grade.

826 Valencia. *642 Things to Write About: Young Writer's Edition*. San Francisco: Chronicle Books, 2014. Author Dave Eggers started 826 Valencia, a nonprofit that runs writing programs for kids. This book offers hundreds of writing prompts meant to inspire young writers.

Hambleton, Vicki, and Cathleen Greenwood. *So, You Want to Be a Writer? How to Write, Get Published, and Maybe Even Make It Big!* New York: Aladdin/Beyond Words, 2012. This book offers practical advice for all would-be writers and includes interviews with best-selling writers as well as successful young authors.

The Learning Network: Teaching and Learning with the *New York Times*—Student Opinion
http://learning.blogs.nytimes.com/category/student-opinion
Each week thousands of kids post their opinions on current events. Learn from some of the best journalists and opinion writers in the world! No subscription needed.

Rookie

http://www.rookiemag.com

This online magazine is the brainchild of Tavi Gevinson, a fashion critic since the age of thirteen! *Rookie* is a place for teenagers to share their opinions on just about anything, from movies to robots to deodorant to hot chocolate.

Scholastic: Write a Book Review with Rodman Philbrick

http://teacher.scholastic.com/writewit/bookrev/index.htm

Author Rodman Philbrick shares his review of Harper Lee's *How to Kill a Mockingbird* and then gives step-by-step advice on how to write a book review.

StoryMonsters Ink

http://www.fivestarpublications.net/storymonsters/reviewers

This website takes submissions from young writers for everything from poems and stories to articles and book reviews.

Teen Ink

http://www.teenink.com

Teen Ink started as a magazine more than twenty-five years ago and has published the work of thousands of teens. Today it also offers a website, books, classes, and many opportunities for writing in all genres!

"200 Prompts for Argumentative Writing": The Learning Network—Teaching and Learning with the *New York Times*

http://learning.blogs.nytimes.com/2014/02/04/200-prompts-for
-argumentative-writing

There's a lot of overlap between opinion writing and argumentative (or persuasive) writing. These two hundred prompts will give you plenty to think about if you're trying to pick a topic.

INDEX

PHOTO ACKNOWLEDGMENTS

The images in this book are used with the permission of: © Robin Nelson/ZUMA Press/Corbis p. 9; © Kris Connor/Getty Images, p. 13; © RosalreneBetancourt1/Alamy, p. 15; © Purestock/ Getty Images, p. 18; © Africa Studio/Shutterstock.com, p. 20; Paramount Pictures/Everett Collection, p. 25; © iStockphoto. com/malerapaso, p. 26; © JupiterImages/Getty Images, p. 34; © Rozaliya/Dreamstime.com, p. 36; © Eric Isselee/Shutterstock. com, p. 40; © Paul Chinn/San Francisco Chronicle/CORBIS, p. 42; © iStockphoto.com/esjessi, p. 44;© koosen/Shutterstock. com (cardboard background); © Everything/Shutterstock.com (spiral notebook); © AtthameeNi/Shutterstock.com (grid paper); © oleschwantder/Shutterstock.com (yellow lined paper).

Cover: © koosen/Shutterstock.com (cardboard); © oleschwantder/ Shutterstcock.com (yellow lined paper).

ABOUT THE AUTHOR

Nancy Loewen has published more than 120 books for children and young adults. Two of her books have been finalists for Minnesota Book Awards: *The Last Day of Kindergarten* and *Four to the Pole* (cowritten with polar explorer Ann Bancroft). Her picture book *Baby Wants Mama* was named an Oppenheim Toy Portfolio Best Book. Loewen has also received awards from the American Library Association, the New York Public Library, and the Association of Educational Publishers. She holds an MFA from Hamline University in Saint Paul, Minnesota. Loewen was born in Mountain Lake, a small town in southern Minnesota. She lives in the Twin Cities. Visit her online at nancyloewen.com.